French Fries

by Joanne Mattern

BLASTOFF! READERS 3

BELLWETHER MEDIA • MINNEAPOLIS, MN

Note to Librarians, Teachers, and Parents:

Blastoff! Readers are carefully developed by literacy experts and combine standards-based content with developmentally appropriate text.

Level 1 provides the most support through repetition of high-frequency words, light text, predictable sentence patterns, and strong visual support.

Level 2 offers early readers a bit more challenge through varied simple sentences, increased text load, and less repetition of high-frequency words.

Level 3 advances early-fluent readers toward fluency through increased text and concept load, less reliance on visuals, longer sentences, and more literary language.

Level 4 builds reading stamina by providing more text per page, increased use of punctuation, greater variation in sentence patterns, and increasingly challenging vocabulary.

Level 5 encourages children to move from "learning to read" to "reading to learn" by providing even more text, varied writing styles, and less familiar topics.

Whichever book is right for your reader, Blastoff! Readers are the perfect books to build confidence and encourage a love of reading that will last a lifetime!

This edition first published in 2020 by Bellwether Media, Inc.

No part of this publication may be reproduced in whole or in part without written permission of the publisher. For information regarding permission, write to Bellwether Media, Inc., Attention: Permissions Department, 6012 Blue Circle Drive, Minnetonka, MN 55343.

Library of Congress Cataloging-in-Publication Data

Names: Mattern, Joanne, 1963- author.
Title: French fries / by Joanne Mattern.
Description: Minneapolis, MN : Bellwether Media, Inc., 2020. | Series: Blastoff! readers. Our favorite foods |
    Includes bibliographical references and index. | Audience: Ages 5-8. | Audience: Grades 2-3. |
    Summary: "Relevant images match informative text in this introduction to french fries. Intended for students in
    kindergarten through third grade"-- Provided by publisher.
Identifiers: LCCN 2019026669 (print) | LCCN 2019026670 (ebook) | ISBN 9781644871447 (library binding) |
    ISBN 9781618918208 (ebook)
Subjects: LCSH: French fries--Juvenile literature. | Potatoes--Juvenile literature. | Convenience foods--Juvenile
    literature. | LCGFT: Cookbooks.
Classification: LCC TX803 .P8 M38 2020 (print) | LCC TX803 .P8 (ebook) | DDC 641.6/521--dc23
LC record available at https://lccn.loc.gov/2019026669
LC ebook record available at https://lccn.loc.gov/2019026670

Editor: Kate Moening   Designer: Jeffrey Kollock

Printed in the United States of America, North Mankato, MN.

Table of Contents

Crispy Potatoes

Heat **wafts** up from your plate.
Warm salt melts on your tongue.
You reach for another crispy,
golden french fry. Crunch!

French fries are made from potatoes. They are often served with hamburgers and hot dogs.

5

The only **ingredients** in most french fries are potatoes, salt, and oil.

How to Make French Fries

1
Wash potatoes and slice into strips

2
Fry in oil or bake in the oven

3
6 Sprinkle with salt

4
Enjoy crispy fries!

fryer

Some people make french fries in a **fryer**. Others bake them in an oven or cook them on the stove!

French Fry History

In the late 1500s, Spanish **explorers** brought potatoes home from South America. But no one is sure who first made french fries.

Some say Belgian **peasants** invented them. Others claim street **vendors** in Paris made the first fries.

Belgium

Paris, France

N
W E
S

Easy French Fries

Have an adult help you make these easy and yummy french fries!

Tools

- potato peeler
- non-stick baking sheet
- bowl
- spatula
- knife

Ingredients

- 1 pound potatoes
- 1 teaspoon salt
- 2 tablespoons vegetable oil

Instructions

1. Preheat oven to 425 degrees Fahrenheit (218 degrees Celsius).

2. Wash and peel the potatoes.

3. Cut the potatoes into strips.

4. Place the potatoes in a bowl. Add vegetable oil and salt. Mix well.

5. Spread potatoes on a non-stick baking sheet.

6. Bake for 15 minutes. Flip the fries halfway through.

7. Turn up the heat to 450 degrees Fahrenheit (232 degrees Celsius). Bake for another 5 minutes until golden.

Thomas
Jefferson

Many people think Thomas Jefferson brought the first fries to the United States. He visited France in the 1780s. Others say American soldiers introduced french fries after **World War I**.

Wherever they began, french fries did not become popular until at least the mid-1800s.

French Fry Timeline

Late 1500s

Spanish explorers bring potatoes to Europe from South America

1780s

Thomas Jefferson visits France and possibly brings a french fry recipe back to the U.S.

1855

A recipe for french fries appears in a French cookbook for the first time

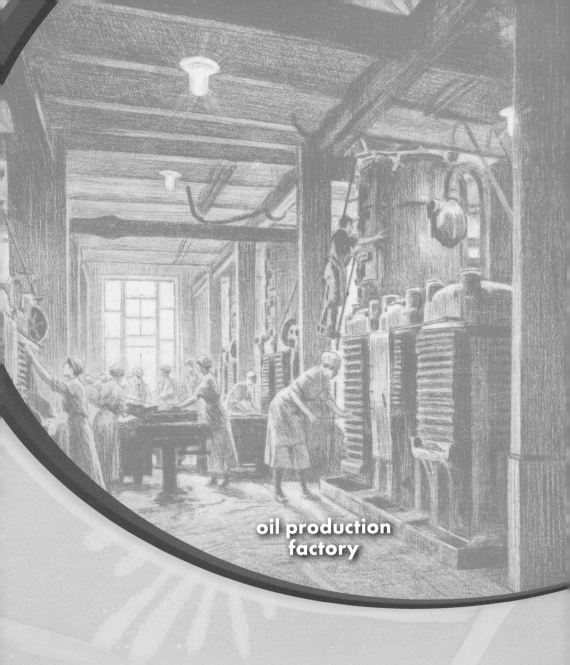

oil production
factory

Before then, oil was very expensive.
When it became cheaper, more
people began to fry their food!

French Fries Today

Today, french fries are all over the world! People eat them in fast-food places and fancy restaurants. They buy frozen french fries to make at home.

frozen french fries

French fries are fun to dip!
Many people dip fries in
ketchup or other sauces.

Some restaurants offer special dips on July 13. That is National Fry Day.

French Fry Shapes

Here are just a few of the shapes french fries come in!

steak fries

waffle fries

shoestring fries

curly fries

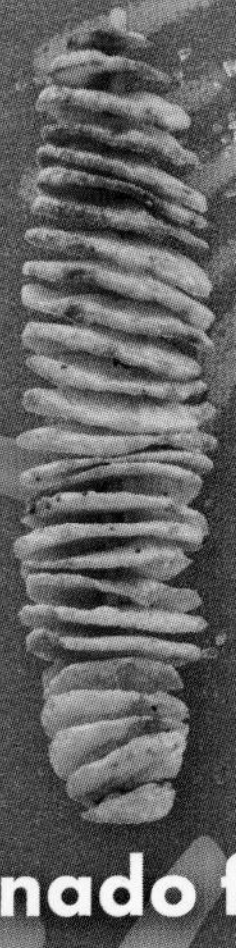

crinkle-cut fries

tornado fries

People enjoy french fries all over the world. Many Belgians enjoy fries with a fried egg on top. In Vietnam, people enjoy fries with butter and sugar.

tornado-style
Vietnamese fries

fish and chips

People in England eat fries with fish. There, fries are called chips!

Not all french fries come from potatoes. Some people make fries from a South American plant called yuca. Others use zucchini, turnips, or even avocados. French fries are tasty in every **style**!

zucchini fries

zucchini

Poutine

People in Canada and the northern United States enjoy a dish called poutine. Ask an adult to help make this recipe!

Ingredients

- 1-2 cups cheese curds
- 1 can gravy
- cooked french fries

Instructions

1. Make french fries following the recipe on page 10.
2. Top the fries with cheese curds. If you cannot find cheese curds, use mozzarella cheese or sour cream instead.
3. Pour hot gravy over the fries and cheese.

Glossary

explorers—people who travel to a place in order to learn more about it or find something

fryer—a large pot filled with hot oil, used to fry food

ingredients—foods that are combined to make another food

peasants—poor farmers or farm workers in Europe

style—the way something is done

vendors—people who sell things

wafts—moves lightly through the air

World War I—the war fought from 1914 to 1918 that involved many countries

To Learn More

AT THE LIBRARY
Bell, Samantha. *Welcome to the Farm: Potato Harvester.*
Ann Arbor, Mich.: Cherry Lake Publishing, 2017.

Love, Carrie, ed. *Food Like Mine.* New York, N.Y.:
DK, 2017.

Ransom, Candice. *French Fries.* Minneapolis, Minn.:
Pop!, 2019.

ON THE WEB

FACTSURFER

Factsurfer.com gives you
a safe, fun way to find
more information.

1. Go to www.factsurfer.com.

2. Enter "french fries" into the search box
   and click Q.

3. Select your book cover to see a list
   of related web sites.

Index